STEP-BY-STEP

PAPIER MÂCHÉ

DERI ROBINS

ILLUSTRATED BY JIM ROBINS

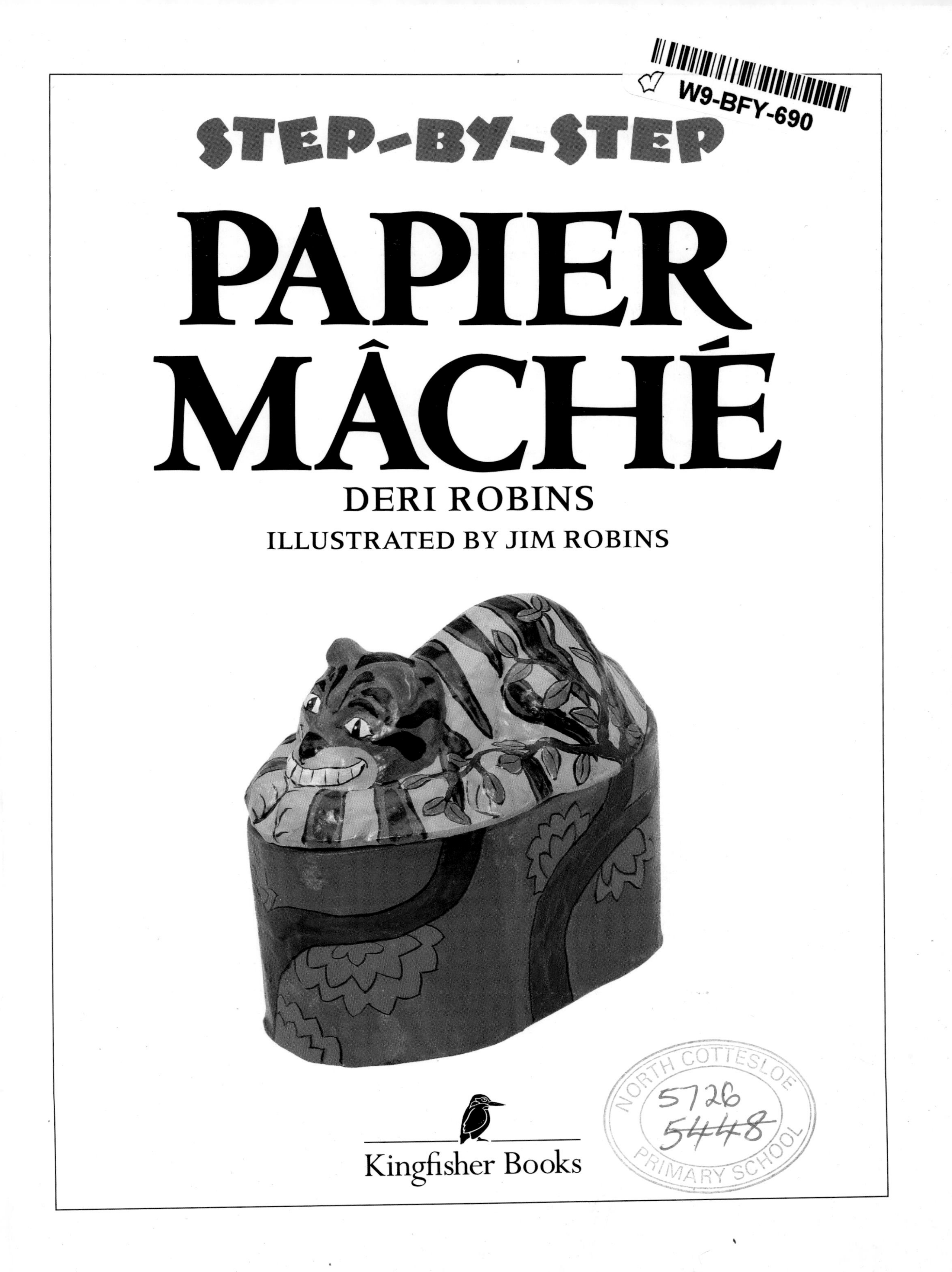

Kingfisher Books

Kingfisher Books,
Grisewood & Dempsey Ltd.
Elsley House,
24-30 Great Titchfield Street,
London W1P 7AD

First published in 1993 by
Kingfisher Books

10 9 8 7 6 5 4 3 2 1

British Library Cataloguing in Publication Data
A catalogue record for this book is available from the British Library.

ISBN 1 85697 1139

Designed by Ben White
Illustrations by Jim Robins
Photographed by Rolf Cornell,
SCL Photographic Services
Cover design by Terry Woodley
Printed in Hong Kong

CONTENTS

Flying Machines 18
Fun Fruit 20
Fruit Hat 22
Helmet 24
Make a Mobile 26
Pirate Puppet 28
Special Days 30
Rose Box 33
Casket & Cat Box 34
Jewellery 36
Spotty Dog 38
More Ideas 40

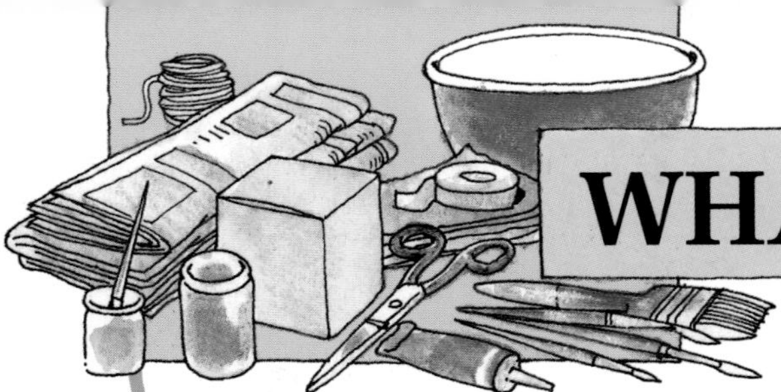

WHAT YOU NEED

Shown below are the main things you will need to make the models in this book. Before you start on a project, check through the step-by-step instructions to make sure that you have any extra items that are not listed here.

Paper

Although you can use many different types of paper to make papier mâché, newspaper is by far the easiest (and the cheapest) to use. Broadsheet papers give better results than tabloids.

Glue and Tape

White glue (PVA) is useful for fixing papier mâché parts together. (It can also be used instead of varnish, for a final coat.) Use masking tape to hold the parts in place until the glue dries.

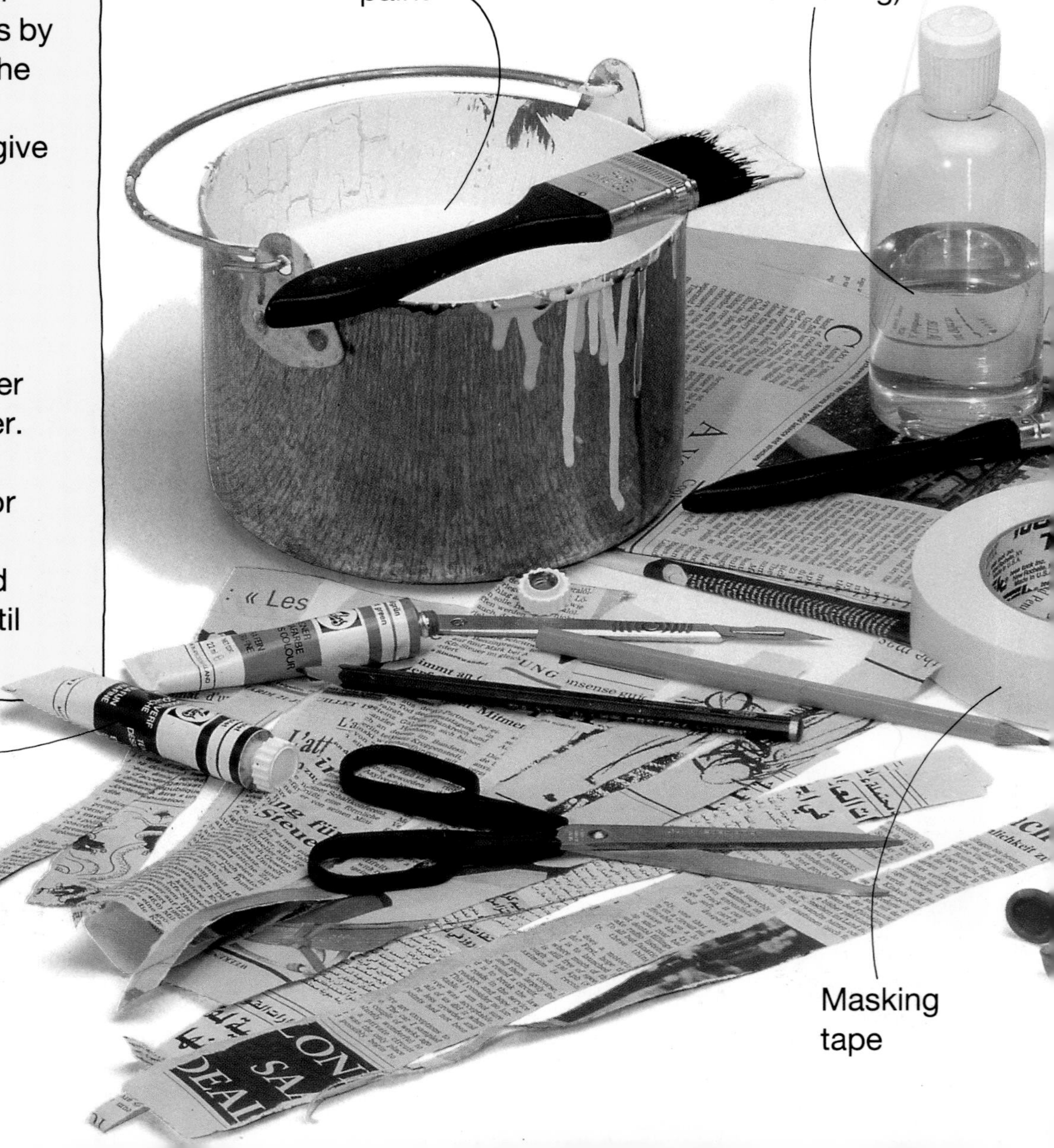

White emulsion paint

White spirit (for cleaning brushes after varnishing)

Gouache paint

Masking tape

Wallpaper Paste

Most wallpaper pastes contain fungicide – this is poisonous, so keep it away from small children, and don't get it in your eyes, nose or mouth! You can also make a homemade paste from flour and water. Heat six cups of water and three cups of flour in a pan. Keep stirring, until it looks like thick custard. Leave to cool.

Junk

Keep a collection of junk, such as cardboard tubes, cereal packets, bottles, string, wire, foil and corrugated paper. For some of the models you will also need some plasticene, and a bag of balloons.

SAFETY TIP:
You will need to use a craft knife to make some of the things in this book. These knives are extremely sharp, so ask an adult to help you.

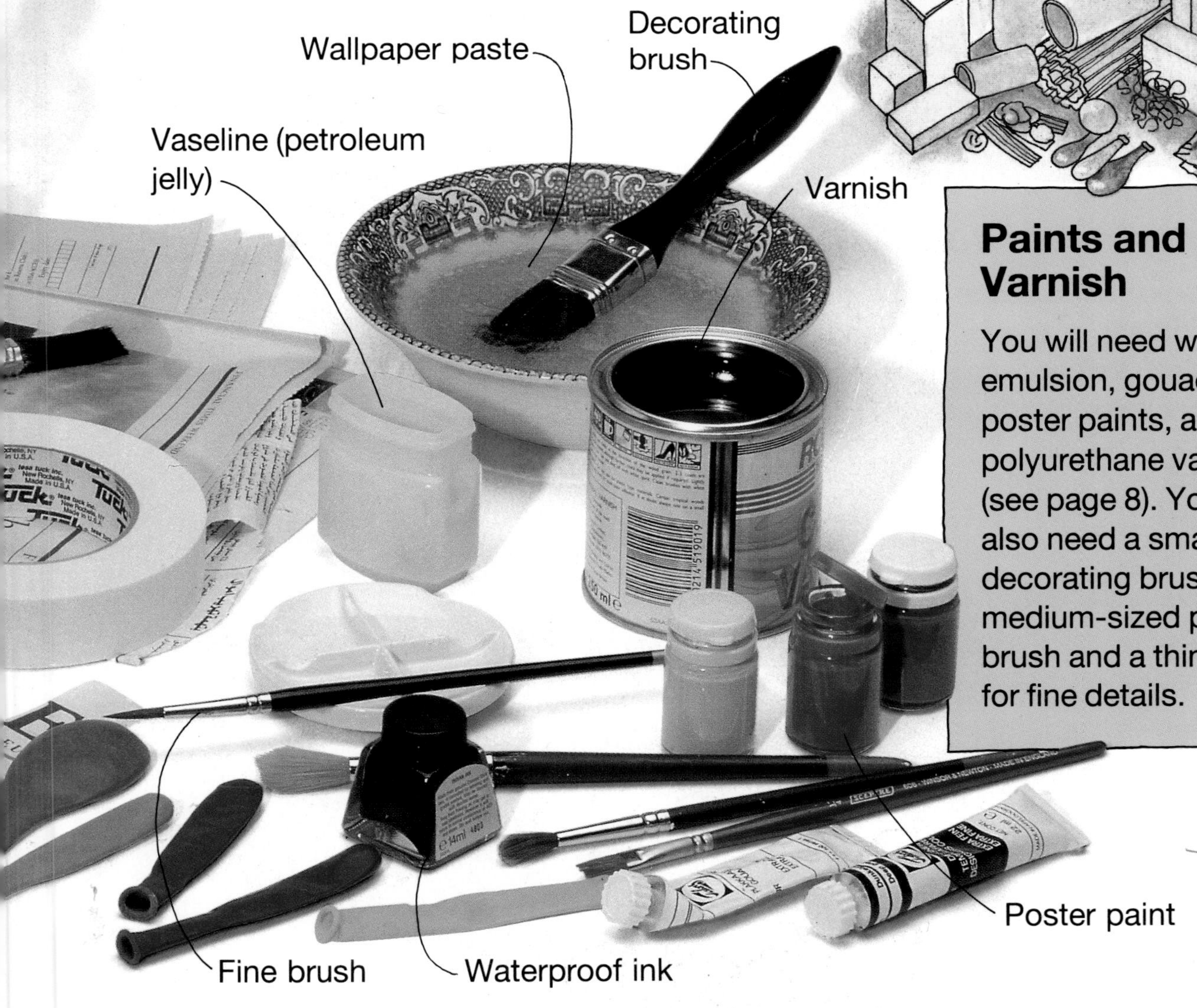

Wallpaper paste

Decorating brush

Vaseline (petroleum jelly)

Varnish

Paints and Varnish

You will need white emulsion, gouache or poster paints, and some polyurethane varnish (see page 8). You will also need a small decorating brush, a medium-sized painting brush and a thin brush for fine details.

Poster paint

Fine brush

Waterproof ink

BASIC TECHNIQUES

Most of the models in the book are made by pasting strips of paper over a *mould* (such as a bowl), or a *framework* (such as a cardboard box). You can also make pulp, which is modelled just like clay.

Using Moulds

Always grease your moulds with lots of petroleum jelly before you put on the papier mâché. This makes the mould much easier to remove later on.

Using Frameworks

Bottles, tubes, boxes and other pieces of junk can be used as frameworks for papier mâché. Unlike moulds, these are not removed when the paper is dry.

Paper Strips

Always tear the paper rather than cutting it – this gives a smoother finish. It's a good idea to work with two piles of different-coloured paper, and to change colour when you start a new layer – this helps you to see where one layer ends and the new one starts.

Pasting Strips

Make up the paste, following the instructions on the packet. Cover each strip with paste, and smooth over the mould or framework. Overlap them slightly, until the object is completely covered. Repeat for all other layers.

Drying Out

When you've put on all the layers, leave them to dry out completely in a warm, dry place – an airing cupboard is ideal. As a rough guide, a bowl made from seven layers of paper will take two to three days to dry out.

These models were all made by pressing pulp into cooking moulds.

Making Pulp

Take eight sheets of newspaper, and tear into tiny squares. Cover with hot water, and leave to soak for 24 hours. Ask an adult helper to boil the paper and water for 20 minutes. Leave to cool. Ask your helper to whisk the mixture with an electric hand whisk. Pour into a sieve, and press out most of the liquid. Add wallpaper paste until the mixture feels like soft modelling clay.

Using Pulp

Pulp can be modelled with your fingers, like clay. It can also be pressed into cooking moulds. Leave to dry out completely – it will take longer to dry than papier mâché that has been made from strips.

DECORATING IDEAS

Bright poster or gouache paint brings papier mâché magically to life! Experiment with colour – bold primary colours and soft pastels both work well, while gold and silver can make a model look as if it is made from metal. Always give your papier mâché a coat of white emulsion before you begin, and finish with at least one coat of polyurethane varnish.

If you don't feel confident enough to paint a design onto your models, try some of the decorating ideas shown below.

Spattering

Paint a base colour over your papier mâché. Dip a used toothbrush or a nailbrush in a second colour. Flick the brush gently with your finger, so that the paint spatters over the surface.

Rag Rolling

Instead of painting your papier mâché with a brush, try dipping a crumpled rag into light-coloured paint and then rubbing it lightly over the surface. Repeat with one or more darker colours for a mottled effect that looks rather like stone (see the Greek urn on page 13). This painting technique is very useful if you want to cover up a bumpy surface!

Torn Paper

Bowls and plates can look stunning if you use torn-up coloured tissue paper or wrapping paper as a final layer. Scraps of silk can even be glued on in this way. You could also try painting on a base coat in the usual way, and decorating with a mosaic made from tiny pieces of cut paper (see page 11).

Découpage

Paint a base colour onto your papier mâché. Cut out pictures from magazines, wrapping paper or plain coloured paper, and glue to the painted surface.

Raised Surfaces

Glue pieces of string, split peas, shapes cut from card, or lumps of pulp onto papier mâché before painting with white emulsion.

BOWLS AND PLATES

Lots of objects can be used as moulds for bowls, plates and trays. As well as china from the kitchen, you could use a football or a blown-up balloon. Use at least seven layers of paper – more if you want your bowl or plate to be really thick and strong.

Cover the inside of a bowl, wok or plate with petroleum jelly. Do the same around the rim and the outside edge.

Paste on at least seven layers of paper strips. Leave in a warm place for three days, or until completely dry.

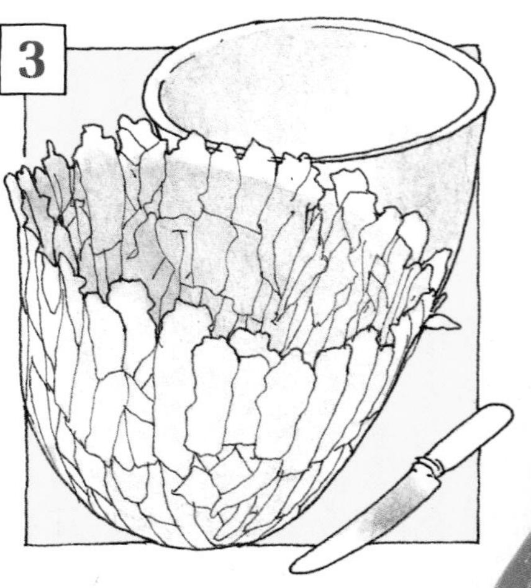

Run a knife between the papier mâché and the mould, and gently ease the papier mâché off.

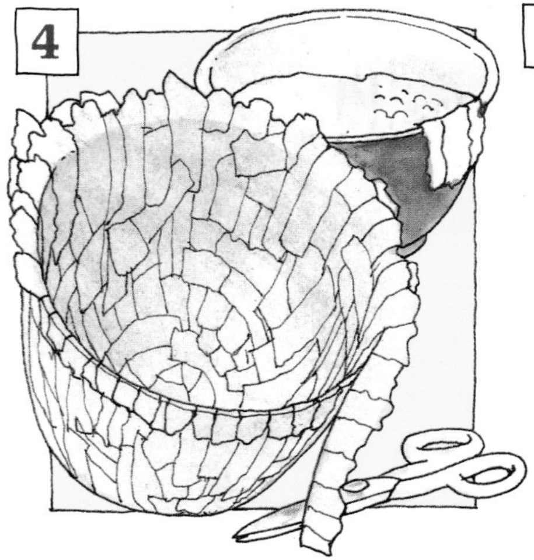

Trim the edges with scissors. Paste over the cut edge with two layers of small strips, and leave to dry.

Paint both sides with emulsion. When dry, paint on your design, or glue on pieces of coloured paper.

Give both sides of the bowl a coat of varnish. This protects the bowl, but doesn't make it waterproof.

Below: The two bowls were both moulded around a wok, while a china mould was used for the plate on the left. The bowl on the right has a mosaic design, made by gluing tiny squares of paper onto a painted background.

Legs and Bases

Glue an empty sellotape roll under the bowl. If you like, you could glue another circle of card under this. Or make feet from small cones (page 14). Cover with two layers of strips.

Making Rims

Coat small strips of paper with paste, and roll up into thin sausages. Bend around the outside of the rim, and hold in place with extra paper strips.

Making Handles

Cut handles from card. Bend back the flaps, and glue to the sides of the bowl. Or make slits with a craft knife, and glue in the ends of the handles. Paper over with strips.

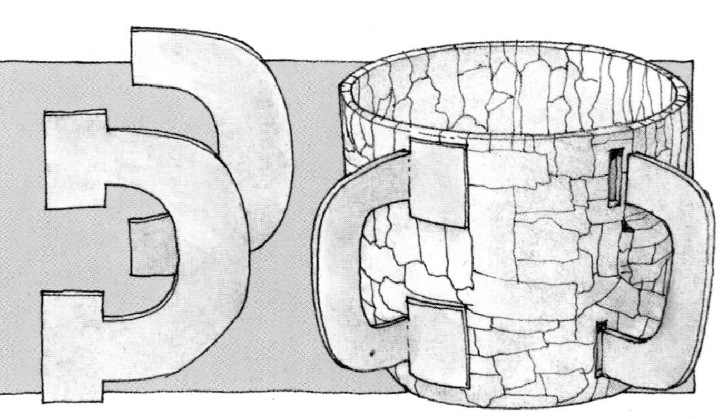

Rolled-up Roses

Make roses by tearing strips of paper, about 25 x 10 cm. Cover one side in paste, and fold in half. Cover in paste again, and roll around the end of a paintbrush to make a rose. Paste onto the side of the bowl, with leaves cut from thick card. Paper over the leaves and the joins with two layers of strips.

The 'Greek urn' was rag rolled (see page 8), and decorated with pictures cut from a magazine. The yellow bowl has legs made from cones of card. The third bowl was decorated with string, painted blue and then and rubbed over with a rag dipped in gold paint.

PIGGY BANK

Balloons are often used as a mould in papier mâché. Here's a piggy bank to make – just add a yoghurt carton for a snout, pieces of card for ears and legs, and a pipe cleaner for a tail. To collect your savings, just cut a hole in the bottom – you could use the plastic end from a packing tube as a stopper.

1

Blow up a round or oval balloon, and cover with vaseline. Paste on five layers of paper strips, and leave to dry for about two days.

2

Cut two ears from card. Draw around a small basin onto card to make two circles, and cut out. Cut each circle in half, and glue into cones for legs.

3

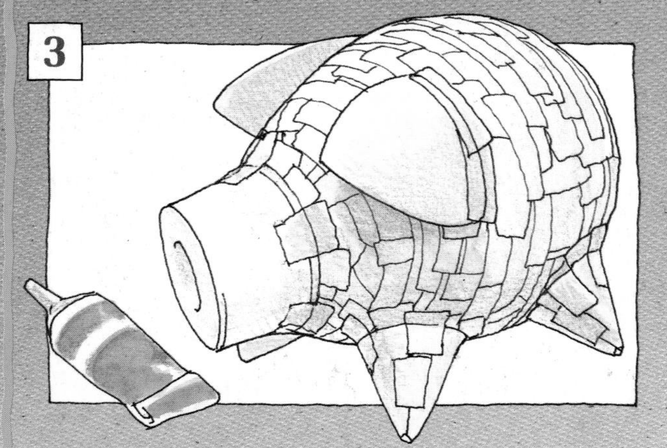

Burst the balloon with a pin, and pull it out. Stick the ears, legs and the yoghurt carton onto the body with white glue. Hold in place with masking tape.

4

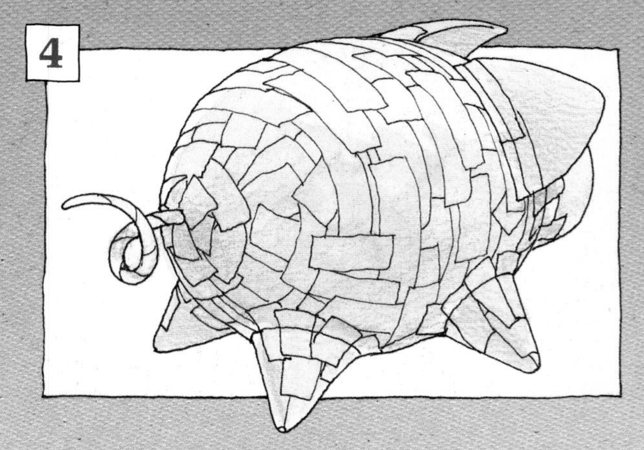

Make a hole in the back with a pin. Bend a pipe cleaner into a curly tail, push into the hole, and glue in place. Cover with two layers of strips.

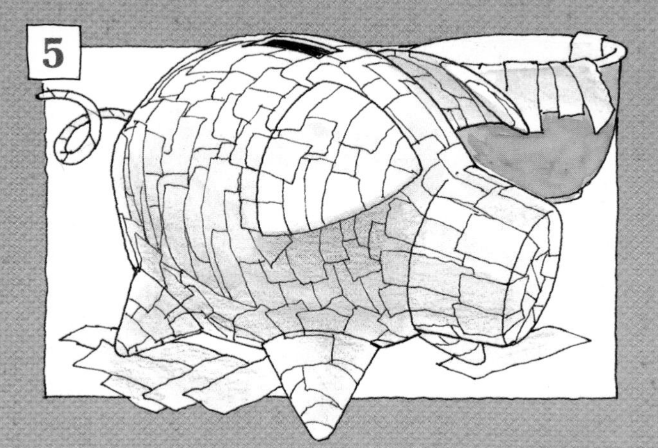

Cover the ears, legs and snout with two layers of paper. Leave to dry. Ask an adult to cut a slit in the top with a craft knife.

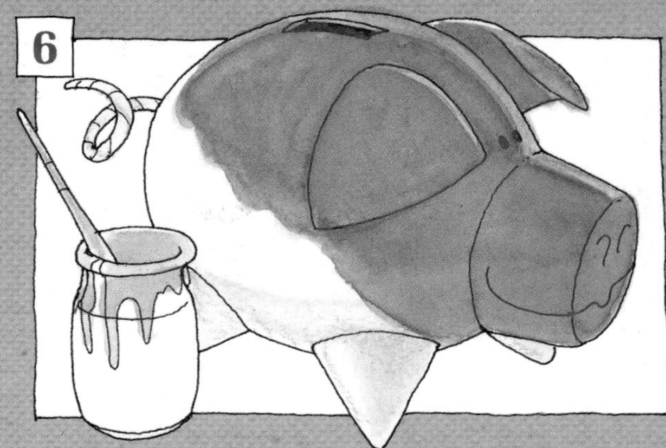

Paint in the usual way. (As an alternative, use pages from a financial newspaper for the final layer, and varnish without painting).

Pigs needn't be pink! Why not decorate with stars, flowers, spots or the owner's name?

MAKING MASKS

All kinds of wonderful masks can be made from papier mâché. Try gluing on string, wool, or kitchen foil – our tiger has ears and a nose made from bits of card, and whiskers made from bristles taken from a brush. A gold glitter pen was used to add shimmery highlights to the stripes.

Blow up a balloon until it's the size of your head. Cover half with vaseline, and paste on five layers of paper.

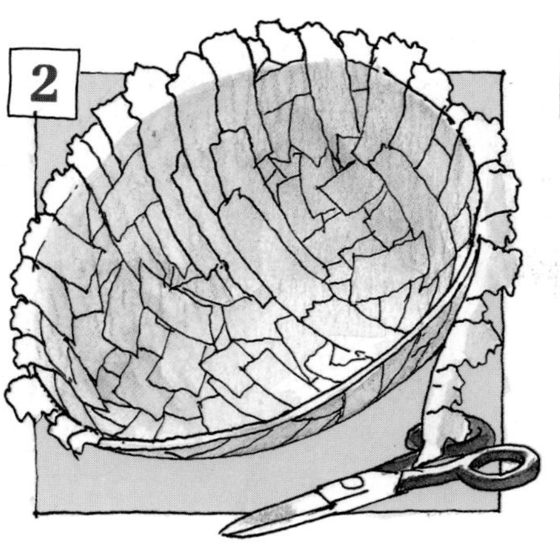

Dry for two days. Take the mask off, and trim with scissors. Ask an adult to cut out the eyes with a craft knife.

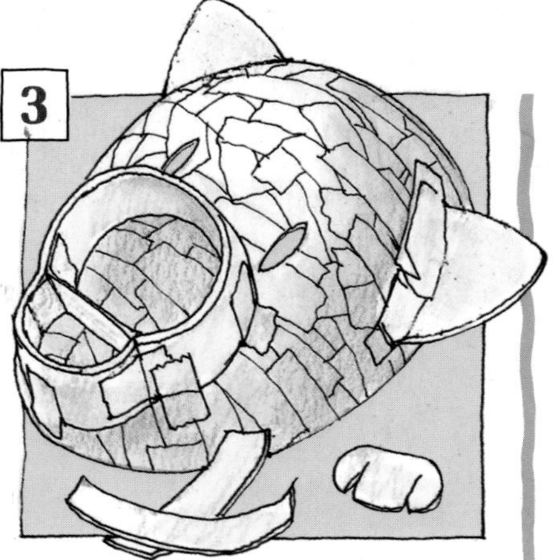

Make the ears and nose from card, and glue to the head with PVA. Tape into place until the glue dries.

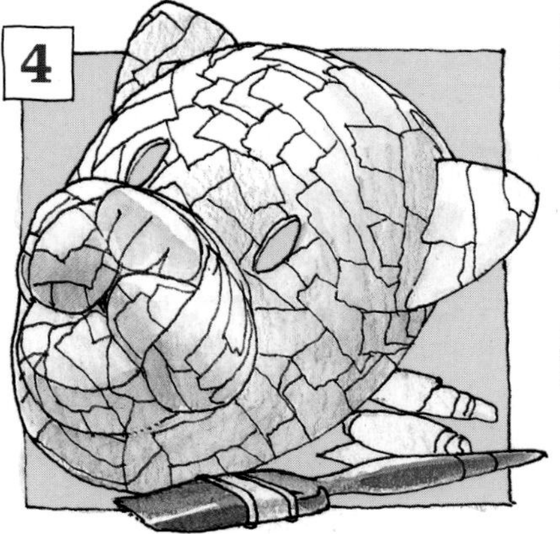

Paste two layers of paper over the ears and across the nose. Pad out the sides with rolls of pasted paper.

When dry, paint both sides with emulsion. Colour with poster paints, and finish with two coats of varnish.

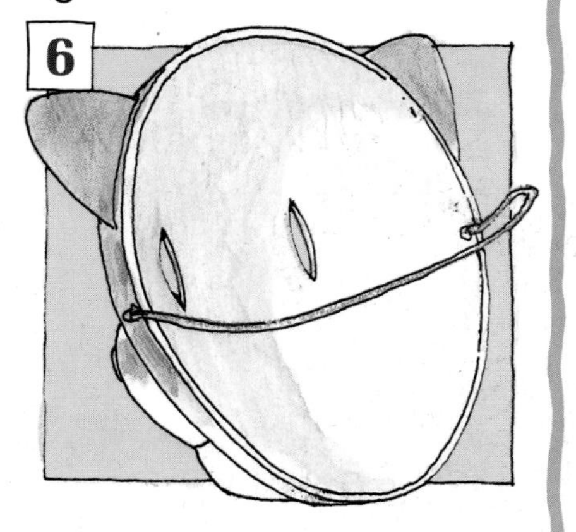

Use a darning needle to make a hole at either side. Thread with elastic, and adjust to fit the size of your head.

Try making scary masks for Hallowe'en, crazy carnival masks, or funny faces for plays and disguises.

FLYING MACHINES

Make hot-air balloons and zeppelins from different-shaped balloons. Paint them brightly, add a coat of glossy varnish, and hang from the ceiling with thread.

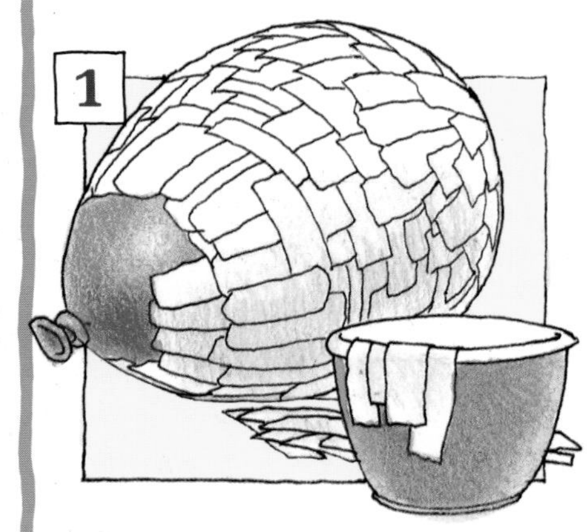

1 Blow up an oval balloon, and grease with vaseline. Cover with six layers of paper strips, and leave to dry.

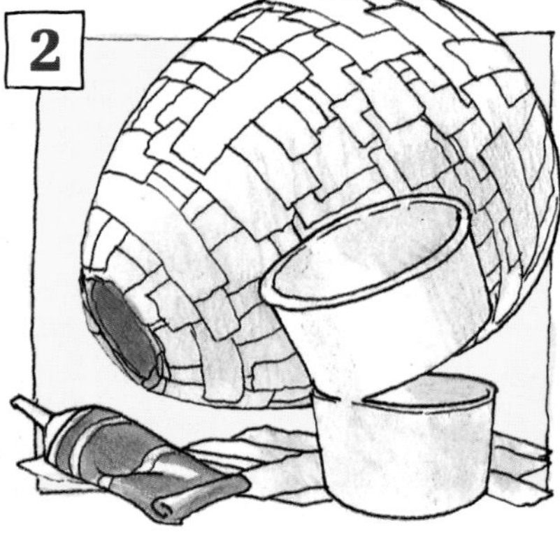

2 Burst the balloon and pull it out. Cut a large yoghurt pot in half. Glue the top half to the end of the balloon.

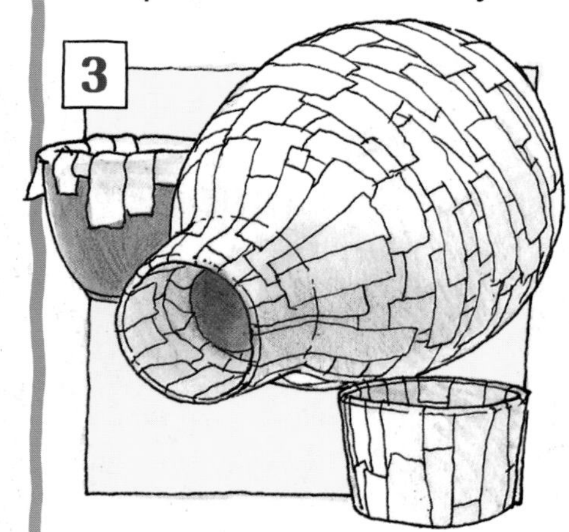

3 Cover both halves of the yoghurt pot with three layers, papering over the join between the balloon and pot.

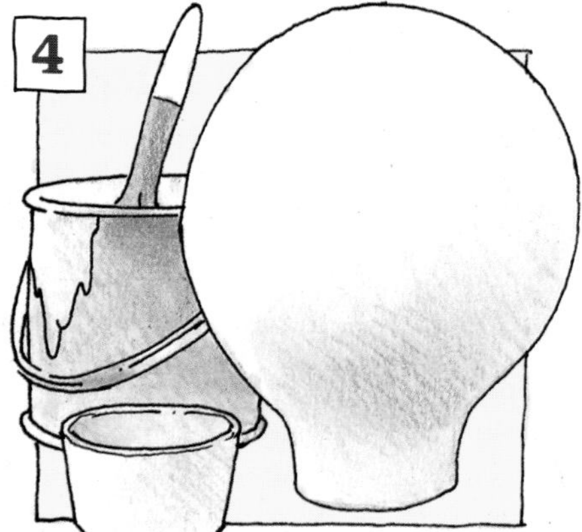

4 Seal the balloon and basket with white emulsion. Paint brightly and finish with a coat of polyurethane varnish.

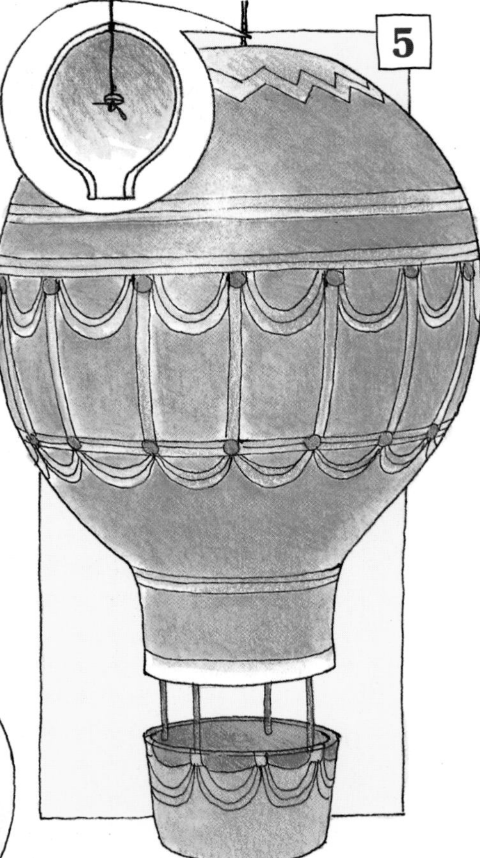

5 Push a threaded needle down through the balloon, and thread on a button. Knot the thread under the button. Pull the button up to the top of the balloon. Attach the basket, using a needle and cotton.

Zeppelin

Cover a long balloon with paper strips. Glue two curved pieces of card together, and support with a strip of card in the middle. Cut a propellor, and attach with a pin.

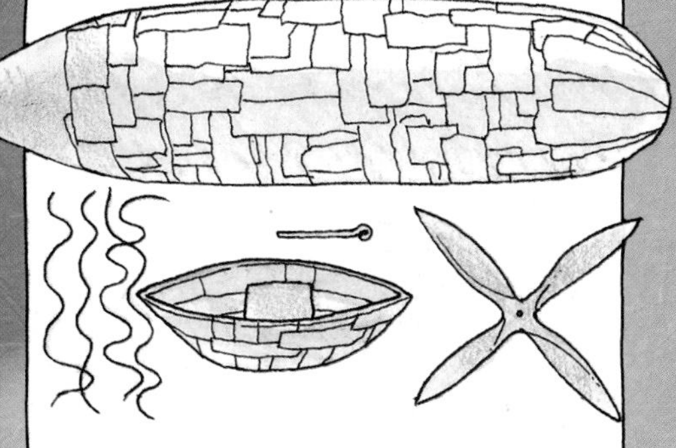

Make a cone from card (page 14), and glue to the nose. Thread two cotton loops through the gondola, and hang them over the zeppelin.

FUN FRUIT

Fill a bowl with fake fruit – or pile up on top of a carnival hat, as shown on page 23. Delicious-looking vegetables can also be made in a very similar way – or how about a plate of sausage, egg and chips?

Bananas and Watermelons

Make a simple framework by taping curved pieces of card together (it doesn't matter if the edges don't meet properly). Paper over with three layers.

Grapes, Cherries and Strawberries

Make these from little balls of paper pulp. When the grapes are dry, glue them in a bunch onto a piece of card.

Oranges and Lemons

Crumple up a piece of absorbent kitchen paper. Wrap another piece around the first one, then add a third and fourth. Use masking tape to mould the paper into the shape you need. Cover with three layers of strips (it's easiest if you let each layer dry before you add the next).

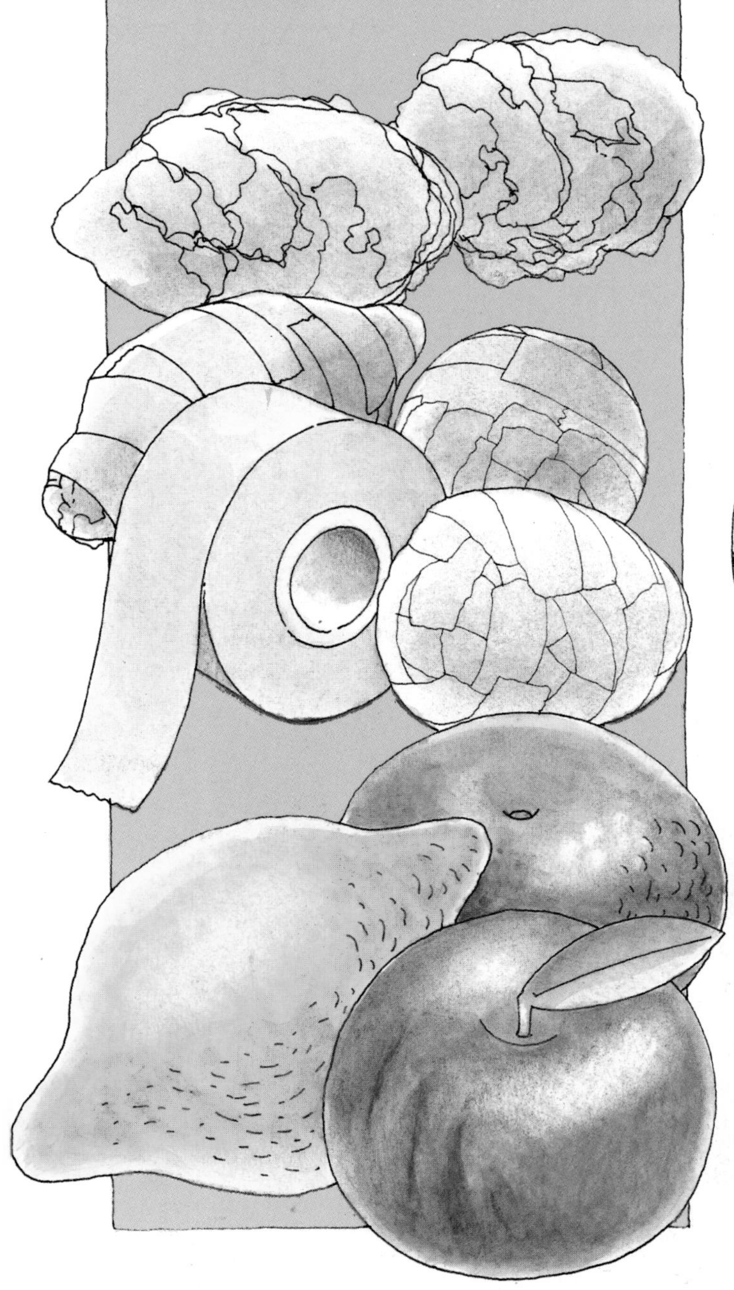

Pineapple

Blow up a small balloon. Cover with seven layers, and leave it to dry. Cut a wide strip of thin card, and cut into pointed leaves with scissors. Glue to the top of the balloon as shown, and paper over the join. Paint the base colour, then the main sections, and finally the detail in each section.

FRUIT HAT

This incredible carnival hat may look top heavy – but as it's made from papier mâché, it's very light and easy to wear.

First, you will need to blow up a balloon until it's the size of your head. Cover with seven layers of paper strips, and leave until completely dry.

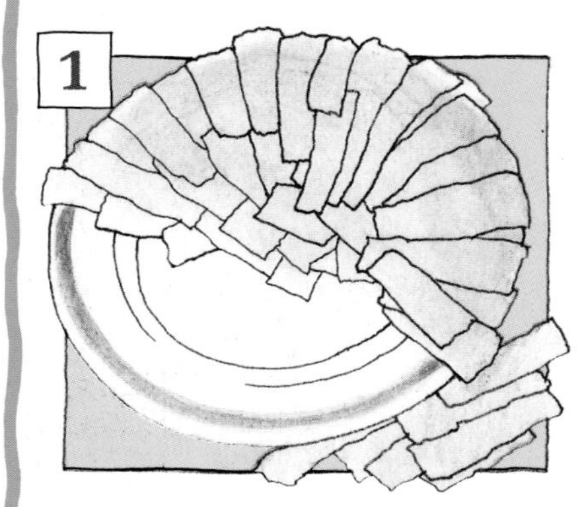

Cover both sides of a paper plate with three layers of pasted strips. Leave to dry.

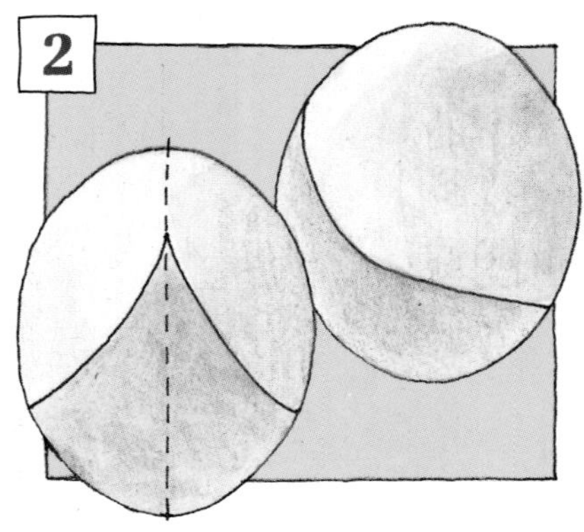

Copy this pattern onto the covered balloon, and cut away the bottom with scissors.

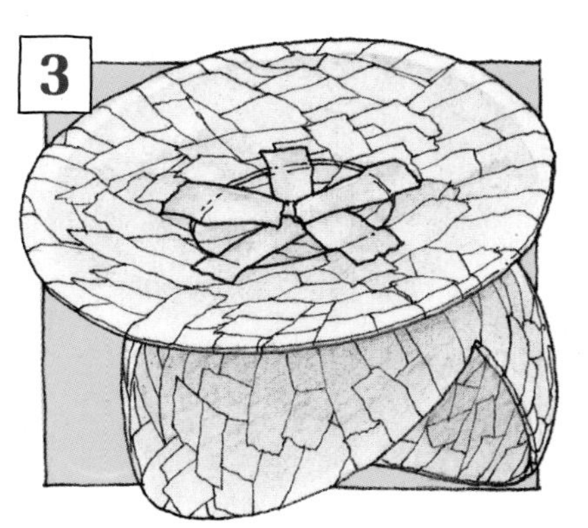

Glue and tape the plate to the hat - this is easier if you cut a hole in the base of the plate.

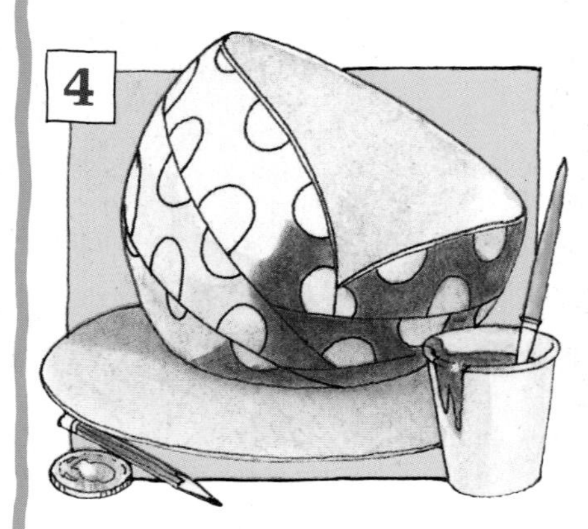

Paper over the join and the cut edges with small paper strips. When dry, paint and varnish the hat in the usual way.

Glue papier mâché fruit, plastic fruit or flowers onto the plate. Hook real or papier mâché earrings (see page 36) onto the hat.

HELMET

Silver poster paint and a coat of matt varnish were used to make this helmet look as if it was made of metal.

1

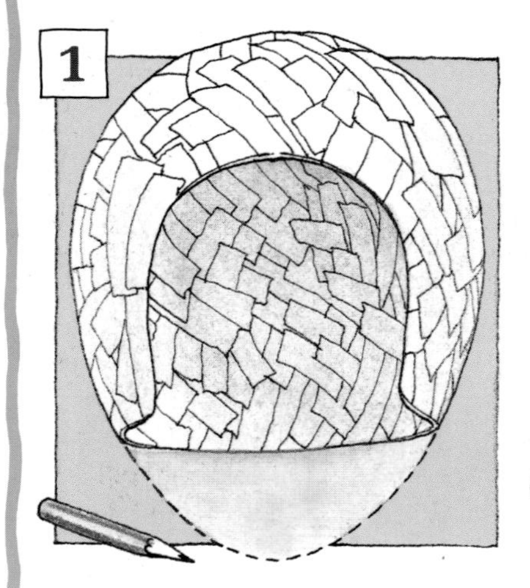

Cover a balloon with seven layers. When it's dry, copy the pattern shown here, and cut out with scissors.

2

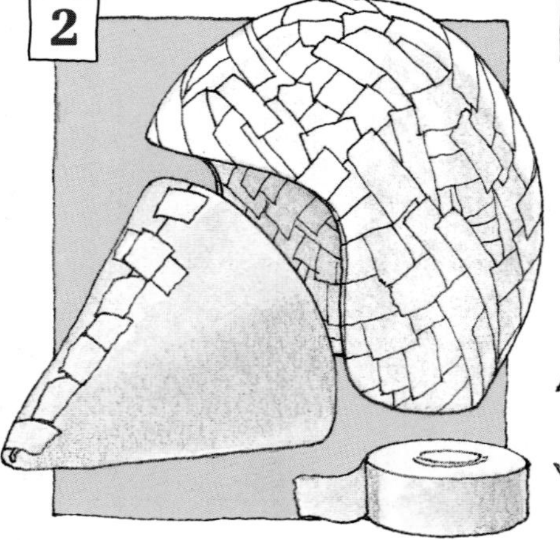

Make a cone from a large semicircle of card. The cone should fit snugly over the front of the helmet.

3

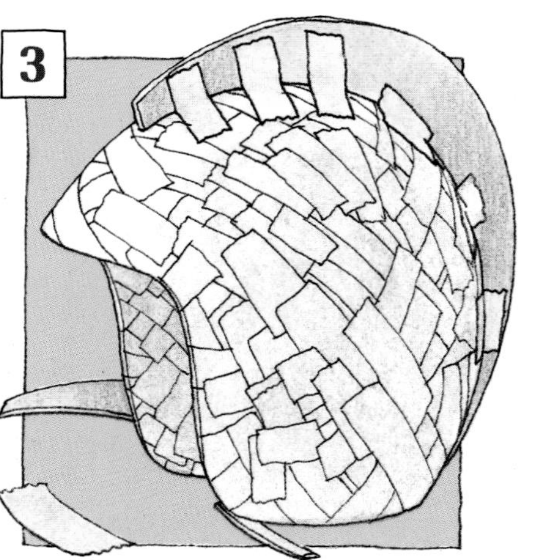

Cut a crest from thick card, and tape to the top. Don't worry if there are gaps between the crest and the helmet.

4

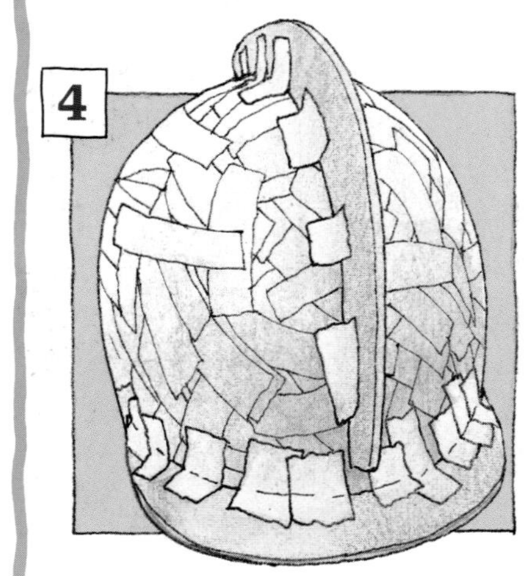

Cut a smaller crescent from card for the back of the helmet, and tape in position.

5

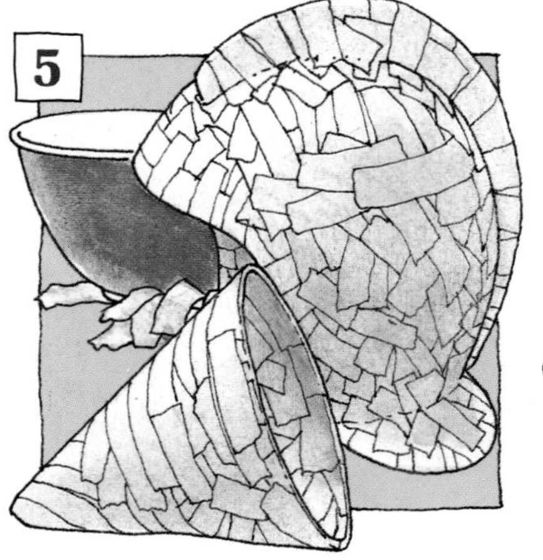

Cover the cone, crest and back of the helmet with three layers of strips. Leave to dry.

6

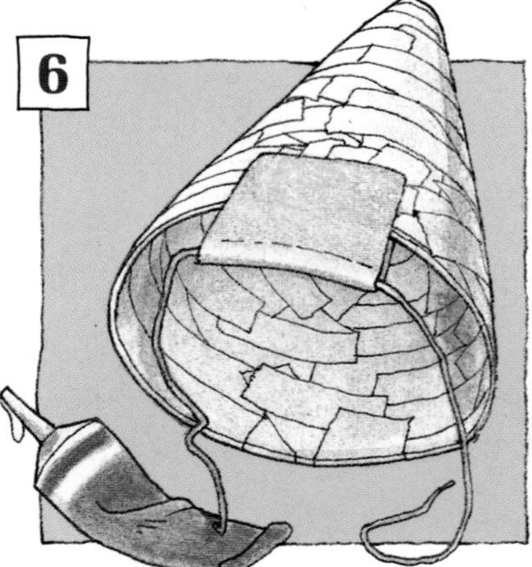

Fold a strip of card in half. Lay a piece of string along the crease, and glue to the cone.

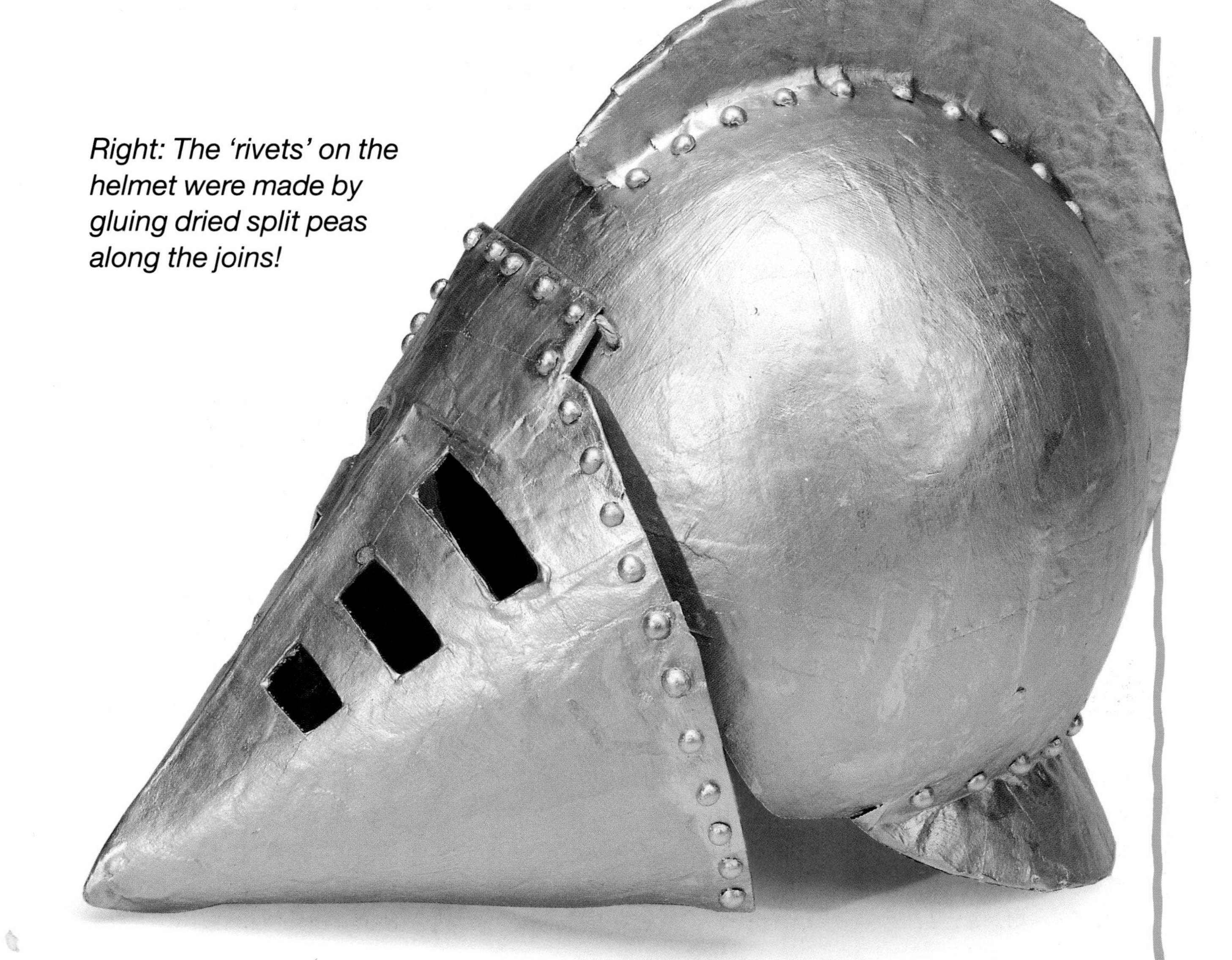

Right: The 'rivets' on the helmet were made by gluing dried split peas along the joins!

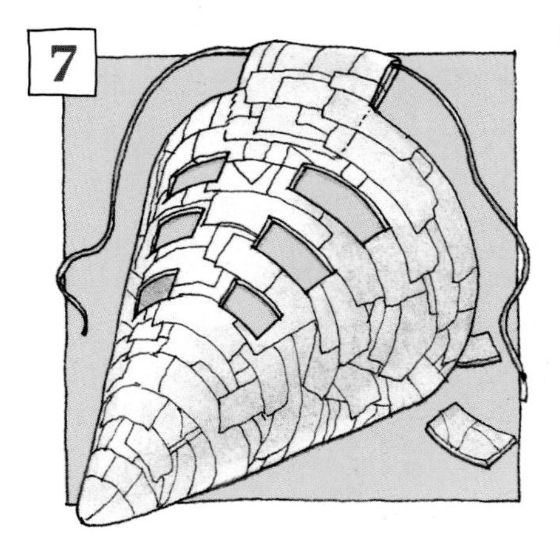

Cover the piece of card with three layers. Cut eyeholes in the cone with scissors.

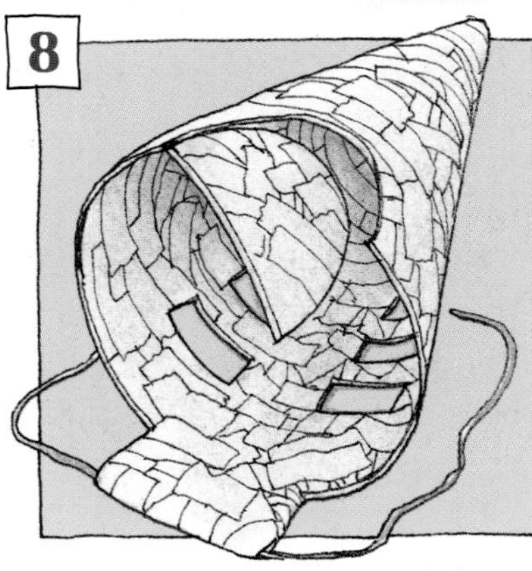

Cut a semicircle as shown, to allow the cone to fit around the chin and neck.

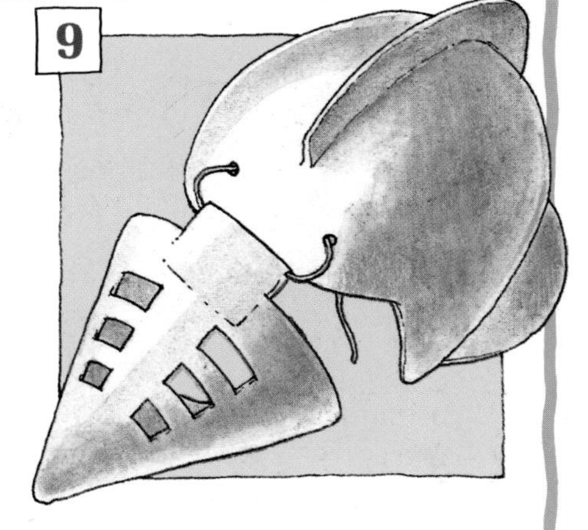

Make two holes in the top of the helmet. Thread through the string, and knot underneath.

MAKE A MOBILE

Papier mâché shapes can be hung with cotton from coat-hangers, or from bars made from dowelling or balsa wood. Hang the mobile up near a door or window, where currents of air will make the shapes spin round.

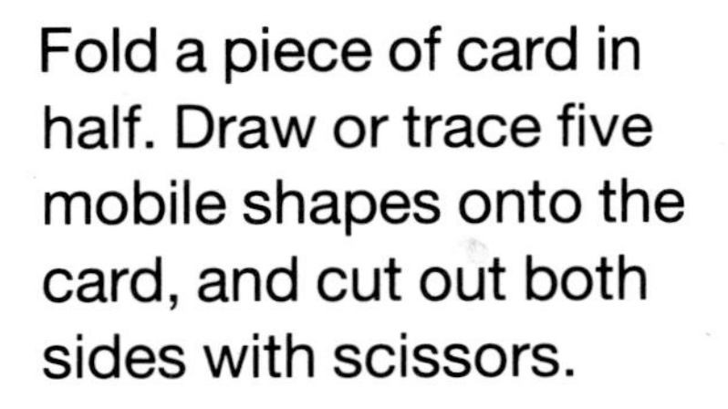

1

Fold a piece of card in half. Draw or trace five mobile shapes onto the card, and cut out both sides with scissors.

2

Staple the tops and sides, and stuff with tissue paper. Staple the gaps, and cover with three layers of strips.

3

Paint and varnish in the usual way. When dry, thread cotton through the top of each shape with a needle.

4

Cut one length of 45 cm and two of 20 cm from balsa wood. Sandpaper until smooth, then paint and varnish. Make holes at each end with a needle.

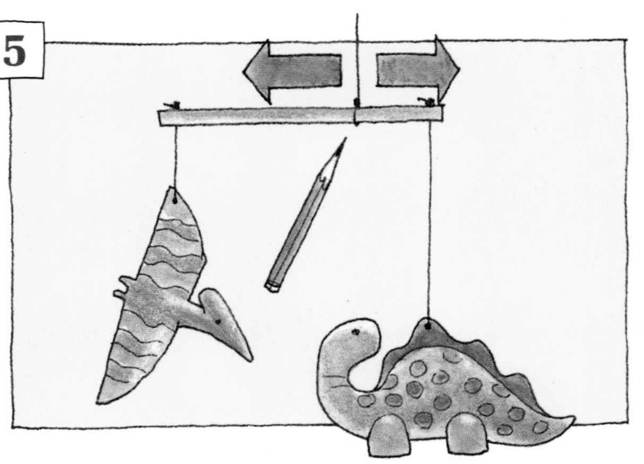

5

Thread two mobiles onto each of the short bars, as shown. Tie a piece of cotton to the middle of the bar, and move it up and down until it balances.

6

Push a threaded needle through this 'balancing point'. Fix the two short bars to the long bar, and add the fifth shape. Hang up from the top bar, finding the balancing point as before.

PIRATE PUPPET

Here's a simple puppet that doesn't need wires or strings – just hold the body under the cloth and wiggle it around! First, blow up a round balloon and cover with six layers of paper.

Once you have mastered this basic shape, you can go on to design a whole theatreful of puppet characters!

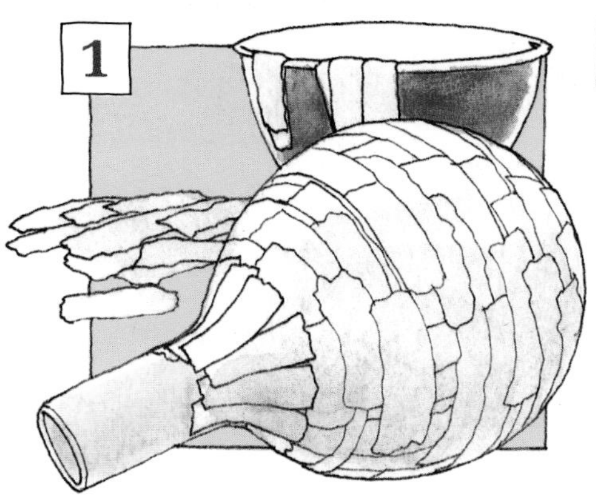

Glue a cardboard roll to the neck. Cover with three layers of strips.

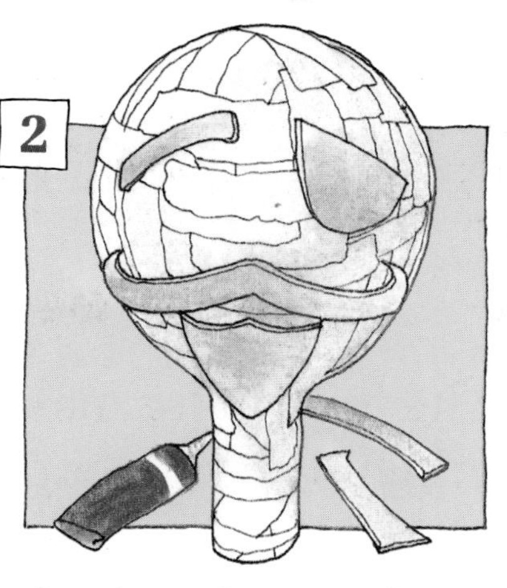

Cut these features from card. Glue on, and cover with three layers.

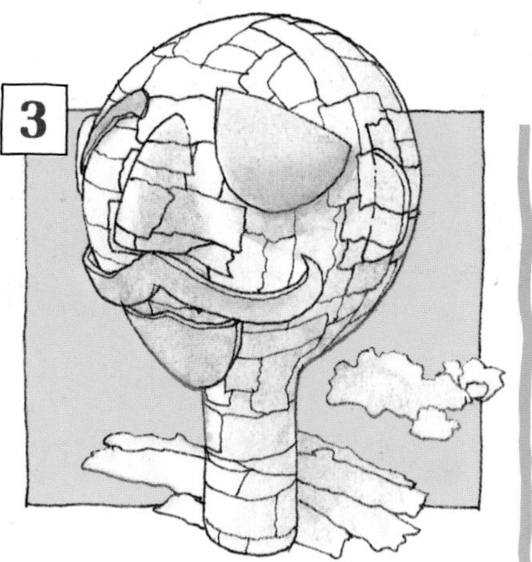

Mould ears and nose from pasted paper strips. Leave to dry.

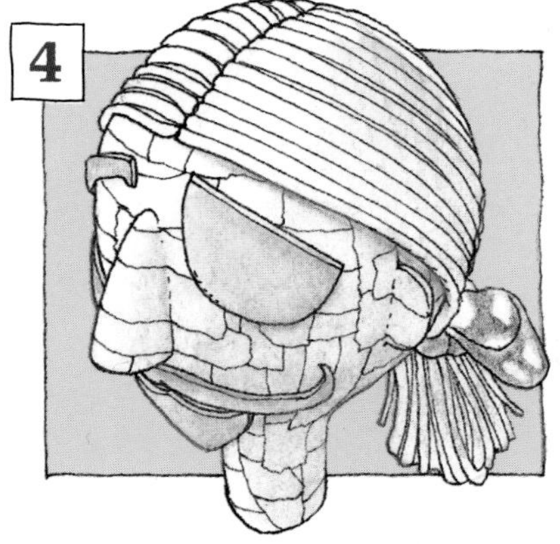

Glue string to the puppet's head. When dry, tie a knot in the back with a ribbon.

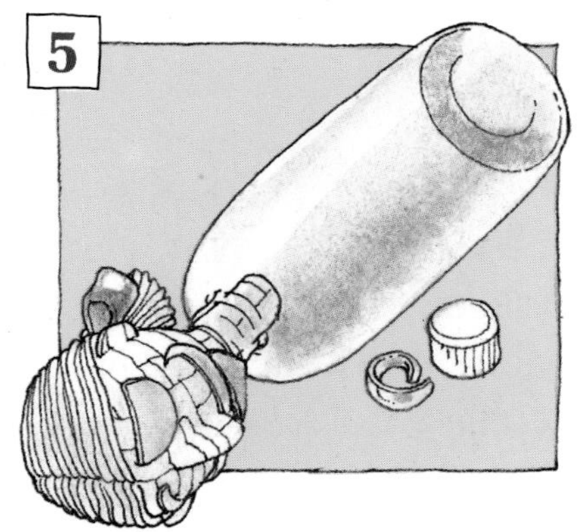

Cut off the top of a plastic bottle, and push in the puppet's head. Fix with glue.

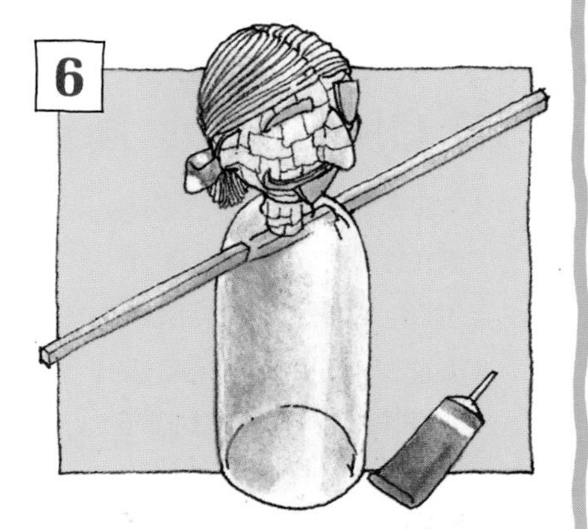

Cut a cross in each side. Push through a piece of balsa wood, and glue in place.

Paint the head, and glue on a scrap of material for a bandanna. Add a gold earring if you have one.

Dress in a child's (or a doll's) T-shirt, or sew two T-shaped pieces of fabric together. Tie a scarf around the neck.

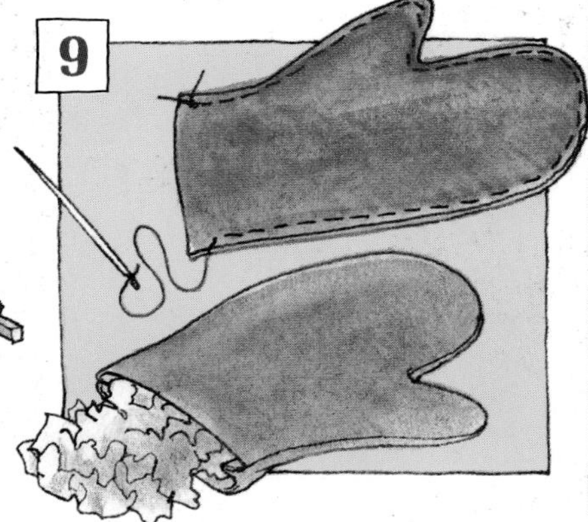

Make two small gloves from scraps, as shown. Stuff with cotton wool, and glue to each of the wooden arms.

SPECIAL DAYS

Lightweight papier mâché is great for making Christmas tree ornaments. Try using gold and silver paint and glitter pens to add a sparkly effect. Over the page, you will also find some ideas for celebrating Easter and Hallowe'en.

A Christmas Angel

Cut the wings from card. Cover with a thick layer of pulp (see page 7). Lay a sheet of clingfilm over the pulp, and roll lightly with a rolling pin. Trim the edges with a knife.

Push a paper clip into the back, as shown, and leave to dry out. Mould the head from a ball of pulp. When dry, glue to the wings. Paint and varnish as usual.

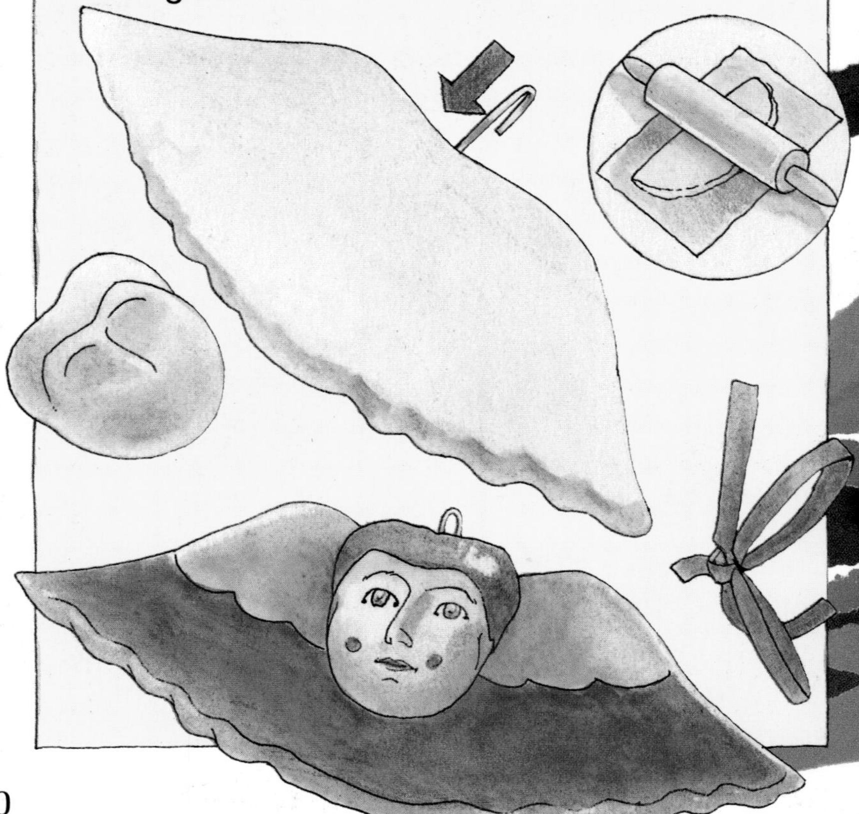

Baubles

Blow up a small round balloon, and cover with six layers of strips. When dry, burst the balloon and paper over the gap. Paint and varnish the baubles, or glue on scraps of wrapping paper. Push an unbent paper clip through the top. and glue in place.

Christmas Shapes

Cut Christmas shapes from thick card, and paper both sides with three layers of strips. Paint them brightly, and varnish as usual. Make a hole through the top with a needle, and thread through with cotton or thin ribbon.

Easter Egg

Cover an oval-shaped balloon with seven layers. When dry, ask an adult to cut it in half with a craft knife. Glue a long strip of card to the inside rim of one of the halves, and cover the rims of both halves with two layers of small strips. When dry, both halves should fit together as shown below. Paint the egg, and varnish.

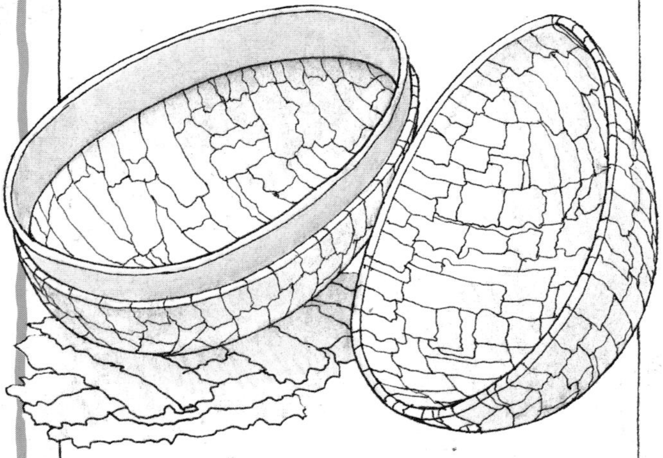

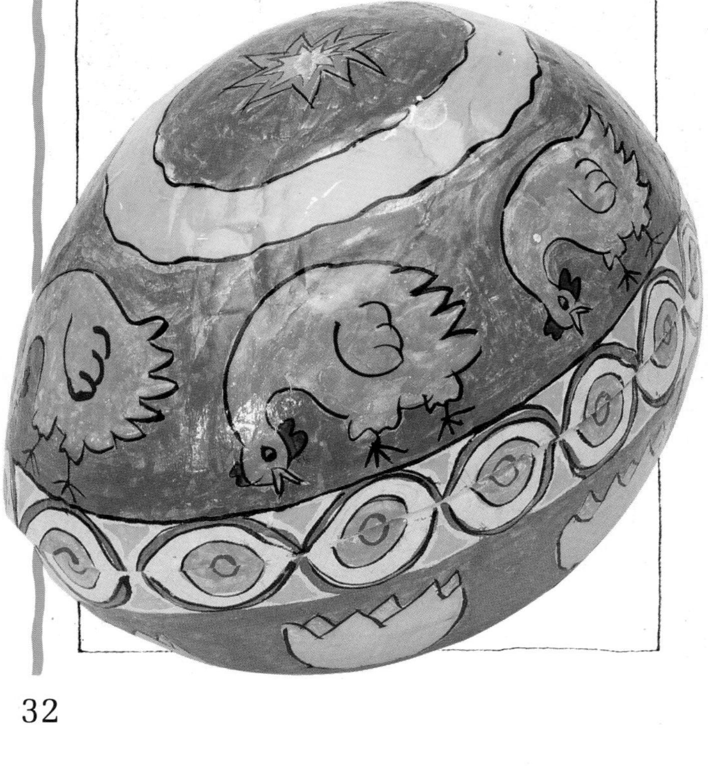

Hallowe'en Pumpkin

Cover three-quarters of an oval balloon with seven layers. Leave to dry. Cut the top of the pumpkin into points with scissors, and ask an adult to cut out the eyes, nose and mouth with a craft knife. Paint bright orange on the outside, and black inside. Varnish, then thread each side with thick cotton.

ROSE BOX

Shoe boxes, hat boxes, tea caddies, chocolate boxes – all these can be transformed by papier mâché!

1. Draw around the box on to some thick card. Add an extra 20 mm all round, and cut out to make a base. Repeat to make a lid.

2. Cut a piece of card, 8 mm less wide and 8 mm less long than the box. Glue this piece to the middle of the lid.

3. Glue the box to the middle of the base. Cover the box and lid with three layers.

4. Add roses and leaves (see page 12) to the box. Paint and varnish.

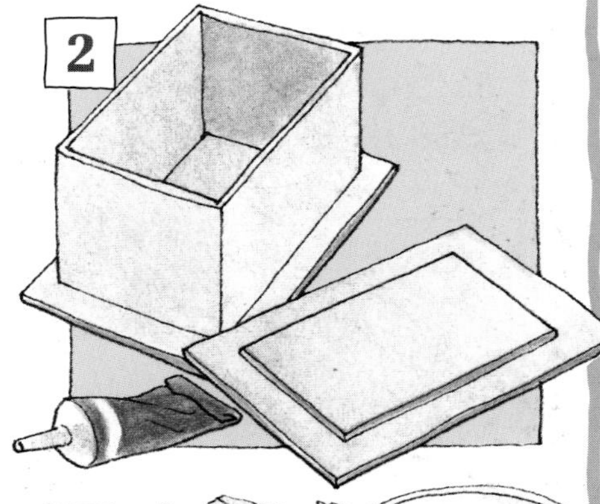

CASKET & CAT BOX

Museums and history books are a good source of ideas for papier mâché. The shape of this casket came from a picture of an ancient Chinese burial urn!

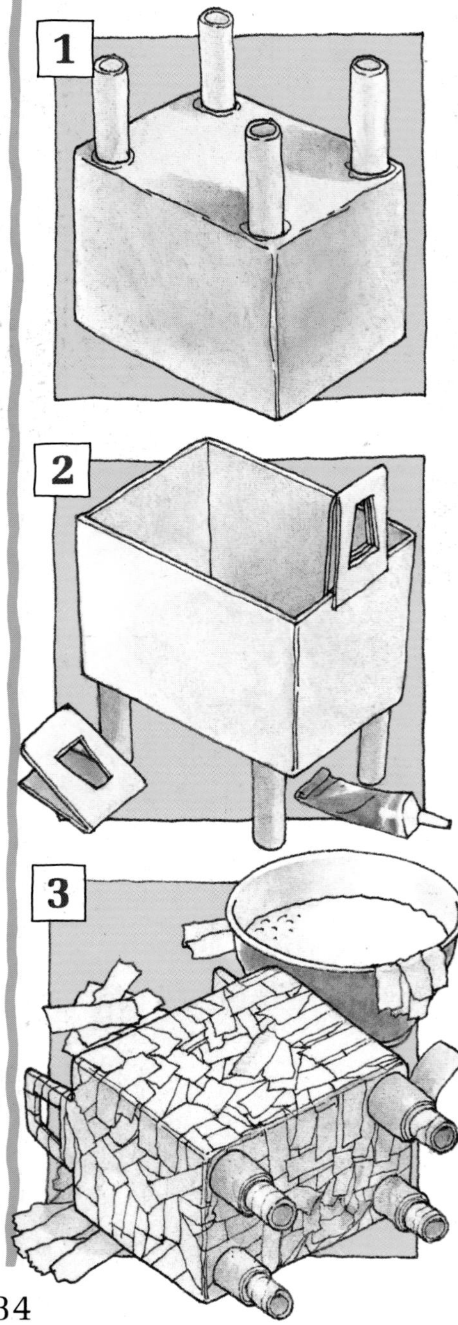

1. Glue legs to a deep box – these were made by gluing thin cardboard rolls to the bottom. You could also make cone legs for the box, as shown on page 14.

2. Glue on handles made from folded card.

3. Cover with three layers, adding more around the tops of the legs. Paint and varnish.

Jelly moulds come in lots of different shapes and sizes. Use them to make great-looking lids for boxes.

1. Grease the inside of the mould thoroughly with vaseline. Press in a thick layer of paper pulp, and leave to dry.

2. Ease out of the mould. Draw around the outline onto card, cut out and glue to the bottom. Cover with two layers of strips.

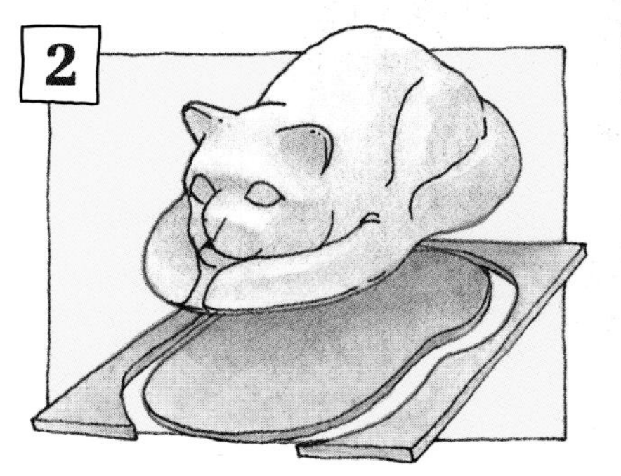

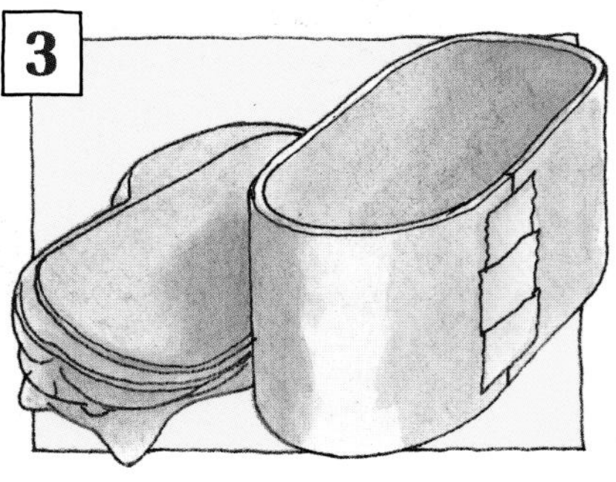

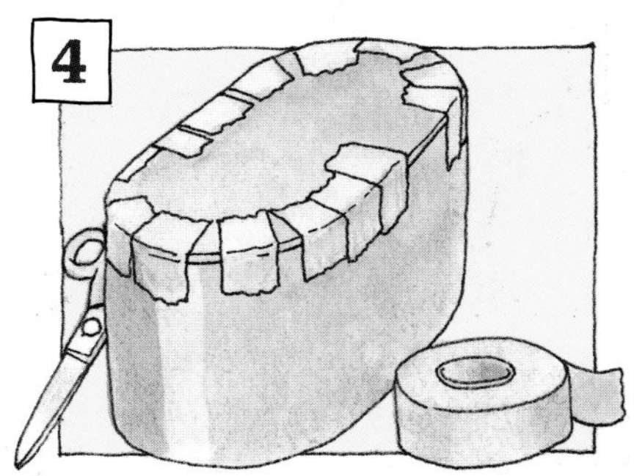

3. Cut a strip of card. Curl it into an oval shape, making it just smaller than the lid. The lid should be able to rest on the top. Tape firmly in place.

4. Cut a bottom for the box from card, and glue and tape in place.

5. Cover both sides with three layers of strips. Paint and varnish.

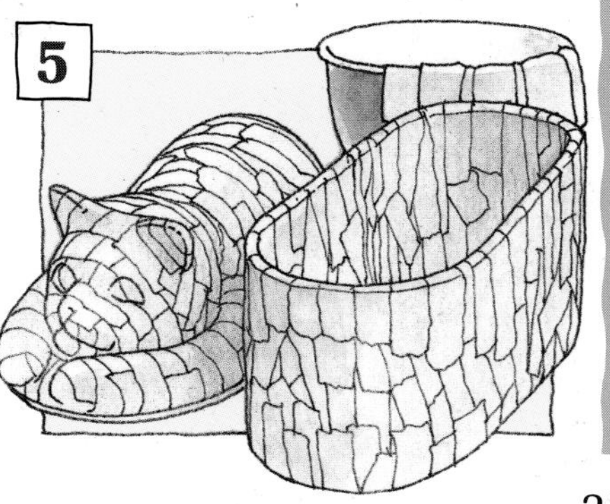

JEWELLERY

Because papier mâché is so light, it can be used to make really large, dramatic pieces of jewellery. The metal attachments (called *findings*) can be bought quite cheaply from craft and hobby shops.

Earrings

Method 1. Cut out shapes from spare bits of papier mâché. For a raised surface, glue on a pattern made from string, and cover with a layer of strips.

Method 2. Cover plasticene shapes with six layers. When dry, take off and trim with scissors.

Glue studs to the back of the earrings, or push through metal hooks. Use tweezers for opening the links.

2

1

Beads

Cut lots of long, V-shaped strips of paper. Cover each strip in paste, and wrap round a knitting needle. Slip off, and leave to dry. Paint, varnish and thread onto cotton to make a necklace.

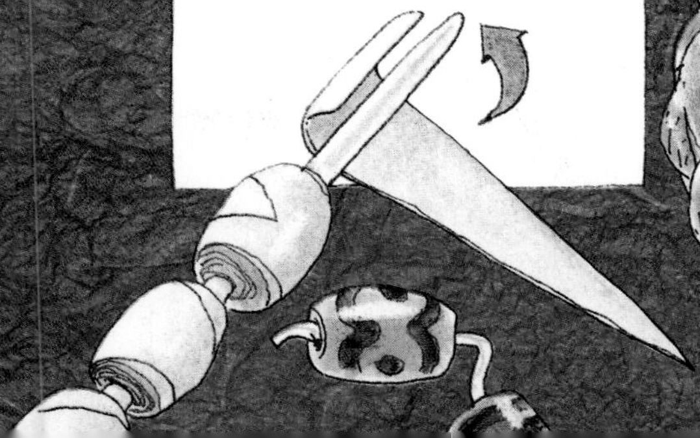

Bangles

Cover an empty sellotape roll with three layers. Glue on dried pasta shells or string. Paint or varnish.

More Baubles

Make huge buttons from papier mâché, or try decorating combs and slides. Use glitter for a sparkly effect – or cover the pieces with scraps of silk or tissue paper.

SPOTTY DOG

This dog's body is made from a large cardboard tube, while the legs are made from smaller tubes. Giraffes, zebras, lions and tigers (in fact, any kind of animal you like) can all be made in a similar way.

1

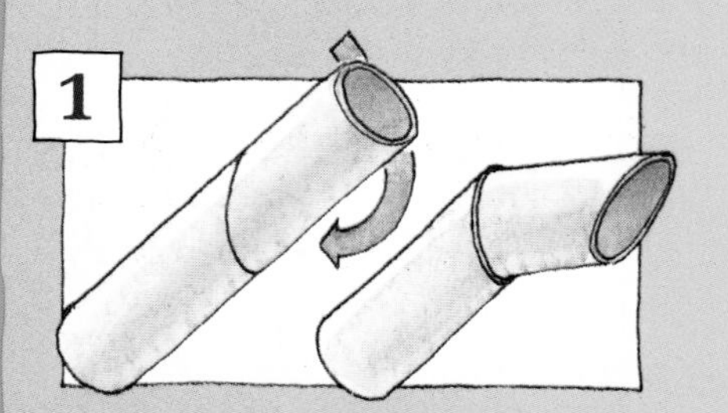

Cut a small tube in half and glue together as shown. Cut the top of the tube diagonally.

2

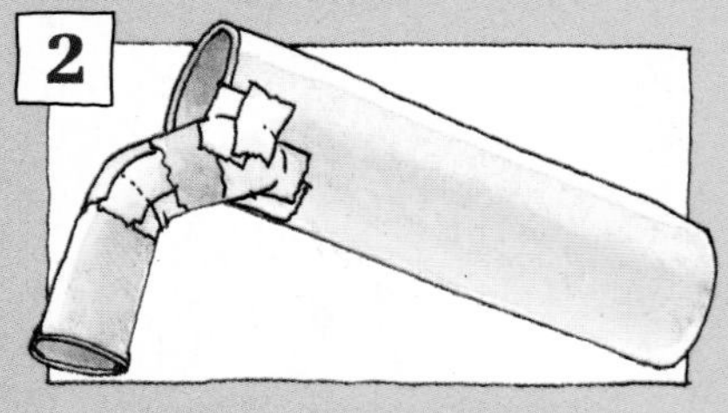

Repeat with a second tube. Tape to one end of the large tube, to make the back legs.

3

Flatten both ends of two more small tubes. Tape them to the front end of the body.

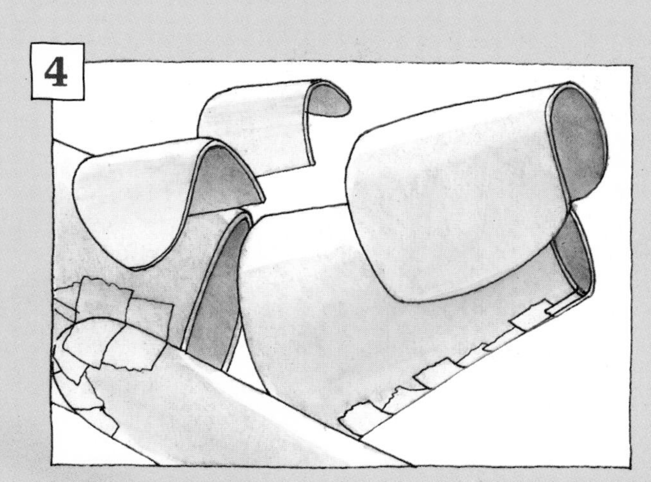

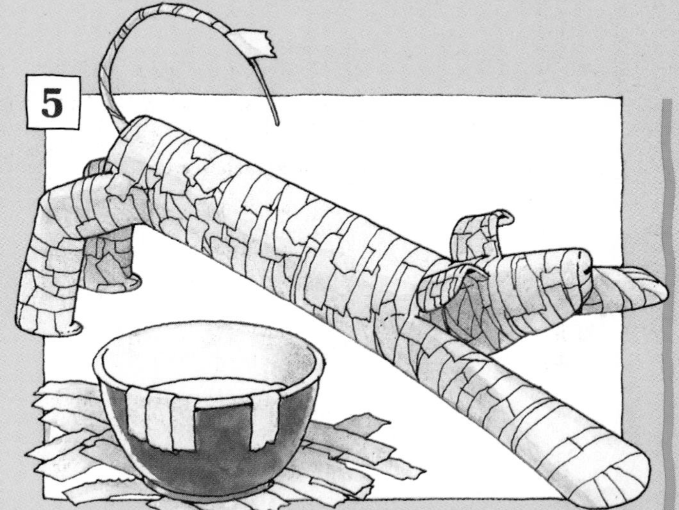

Glue a yoghurt carton, or a cone made from card, to the front of the tube. Cut a flap for the muzzle as shown, and glue to the head. Add ears made from card.

Cut small circles and glue under the back legs to make paws. Cover the dog with four layers of papier mâché. Add extra strips around the joins, and around the big tube to pad out the shape. Push in a tail made from garden wire, and cover in three layers of strips. When dry, paint and varnish in the usual way.

MORE IDEAS

Try making some small toys from papier mâché – mould the shapes from plasticene, and cover them with six layers of tiny paper strips. When dry, cut in half and take off the mould. Glue the halves back together, and paint. Old bath toys, like the duck on the right, also make good moulds...

For jointed toys (like the bear shown above on the left), make the limbs and the body separately. Link to the body with a needle threaded with elastic...

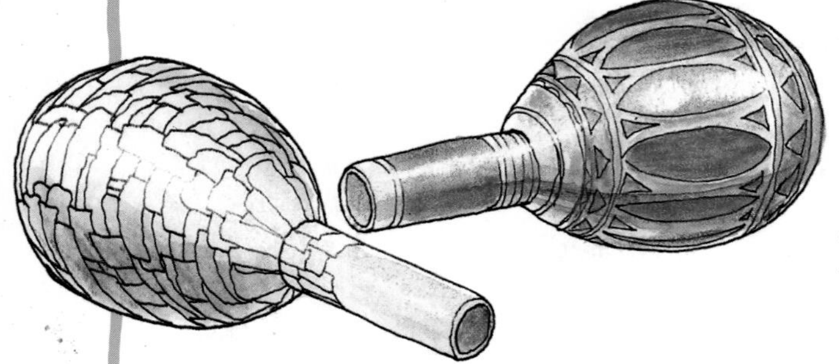

Use balloons and cardboard tubes to make maracas like the ones on the left! Fill with dried peas or beans...

Large cardboard boxes can be turned into fantasy buildings with papier mâché. By adding 'extras' made from pieces of card, you could make a castle, a garage, or even a whole doll's house. Make furniture from tubes of card, matchboxes and other scraps.